RUNNERS COLORING BOOK

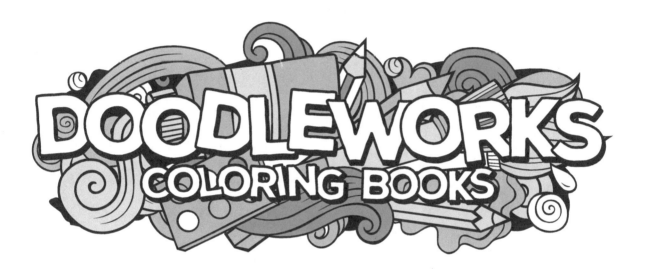

To view our full range of books search for

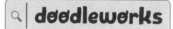

on Amazon.

Copyright © 2019 Doodleworks Coloring Books.
All Rights Reserved. ISBN: 9781656811806

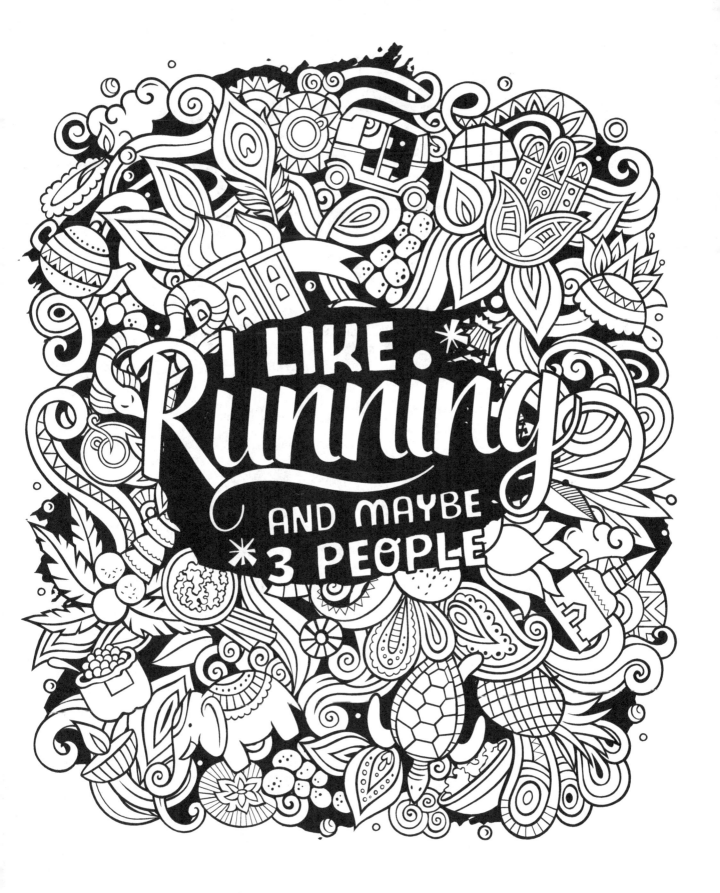

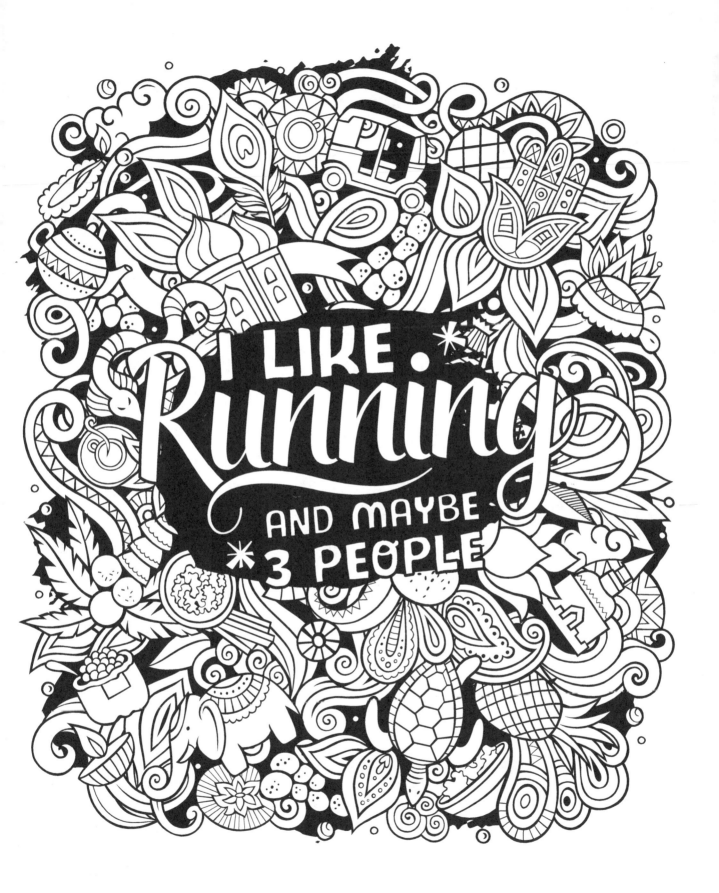

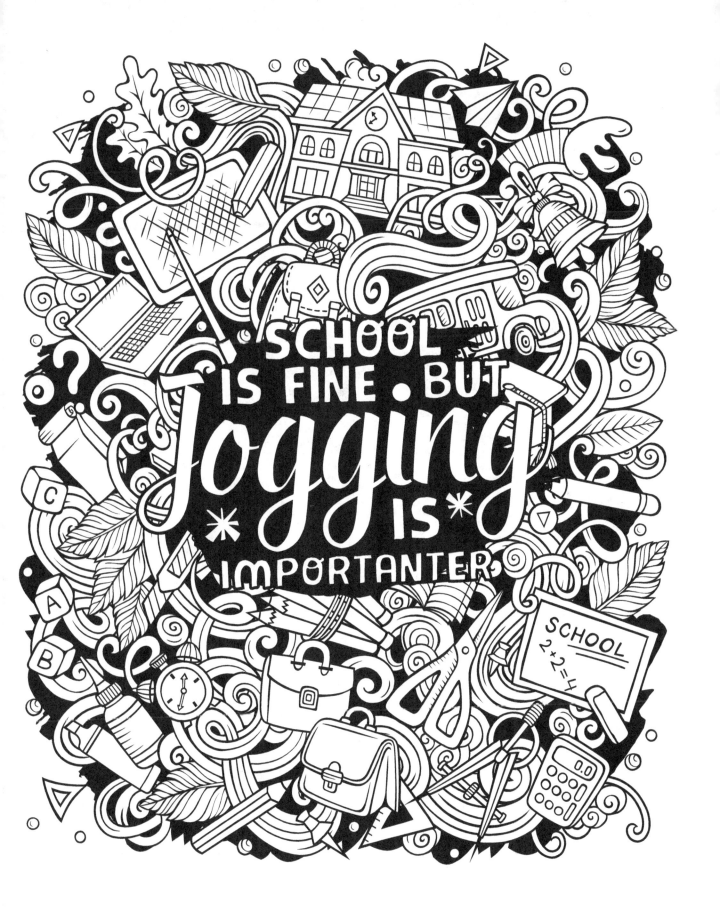

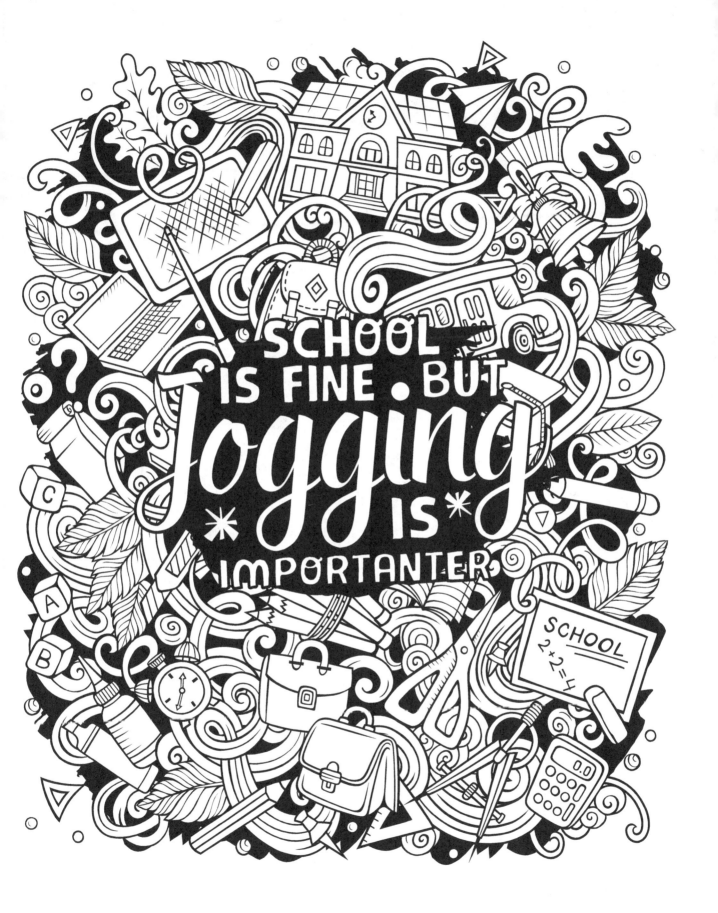

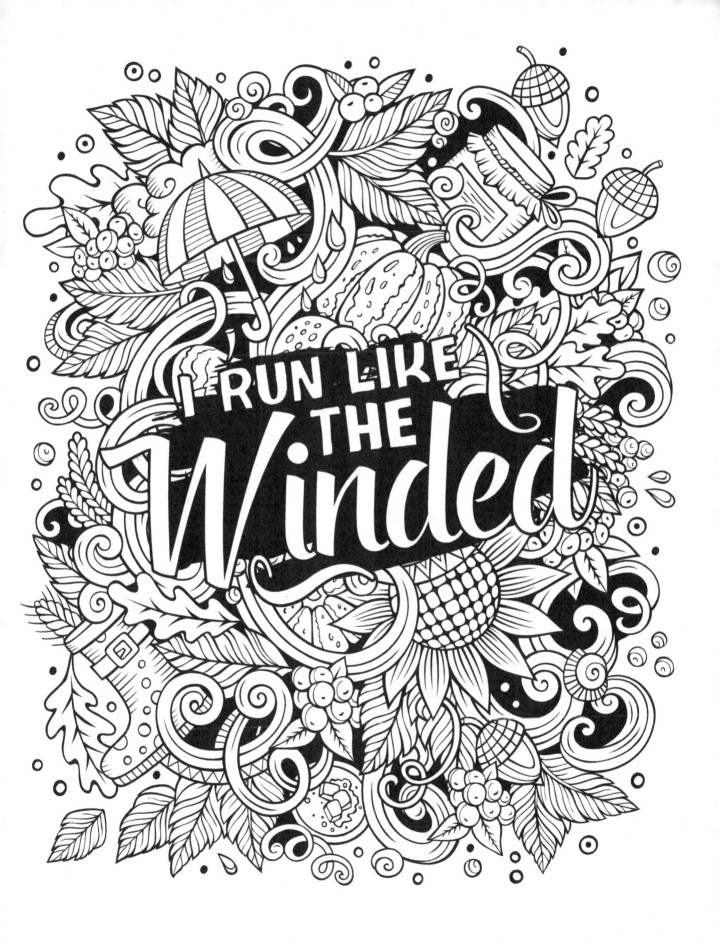

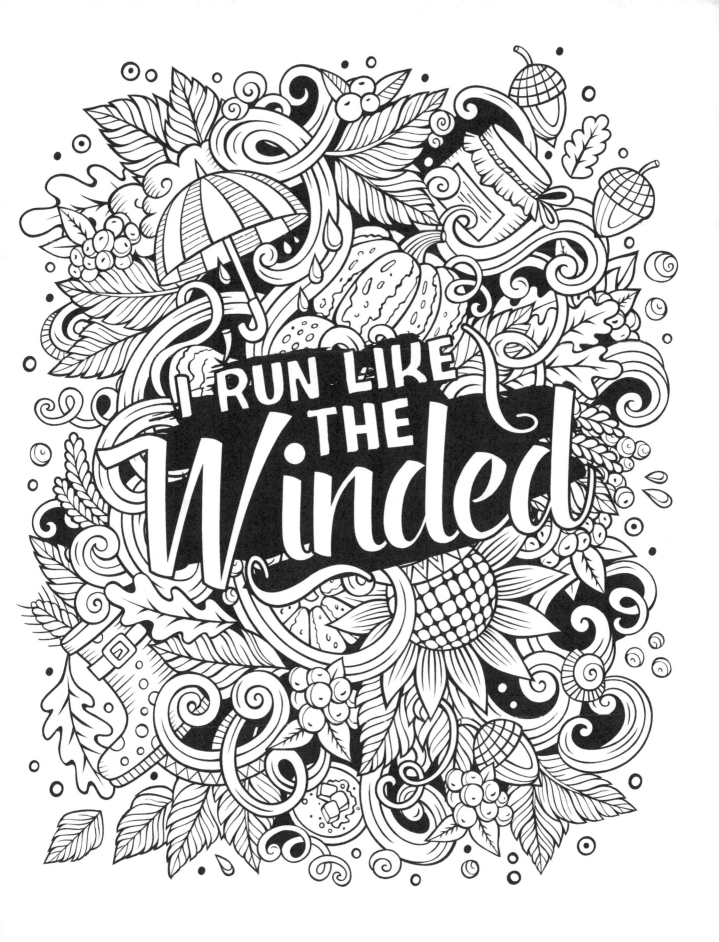

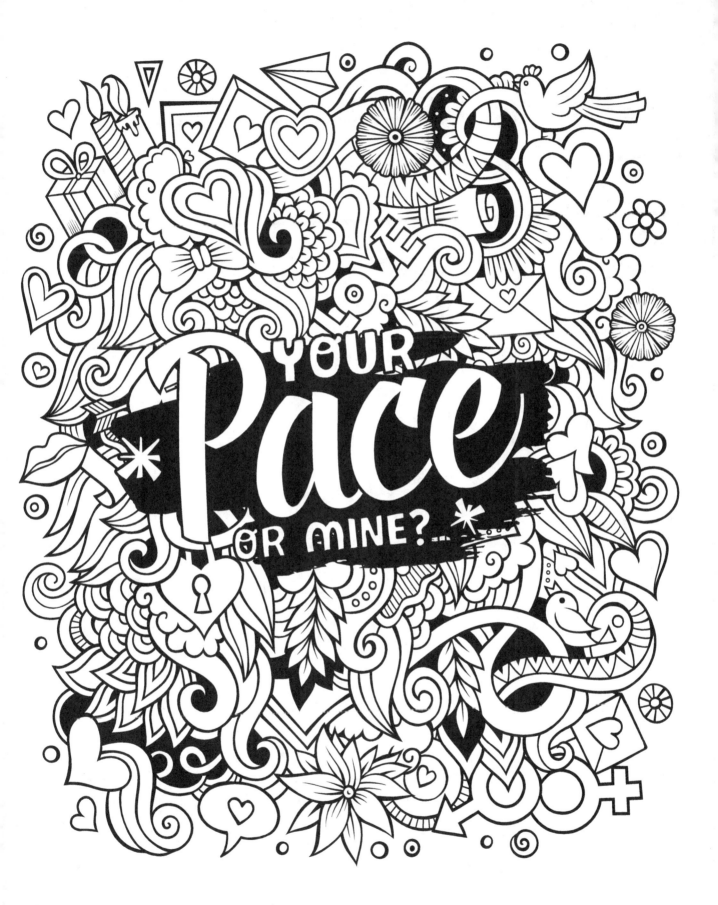

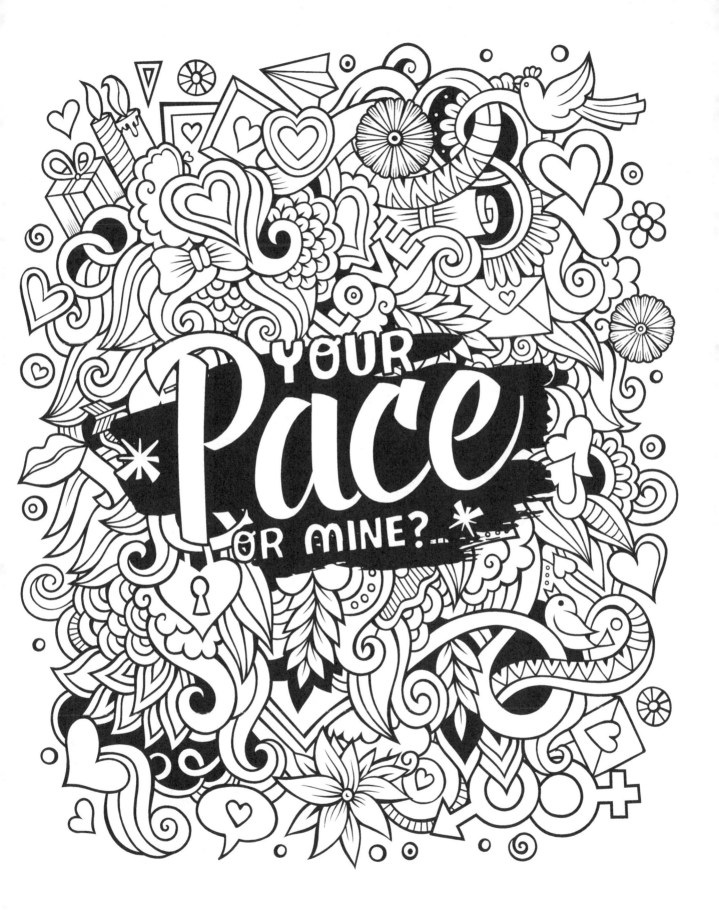

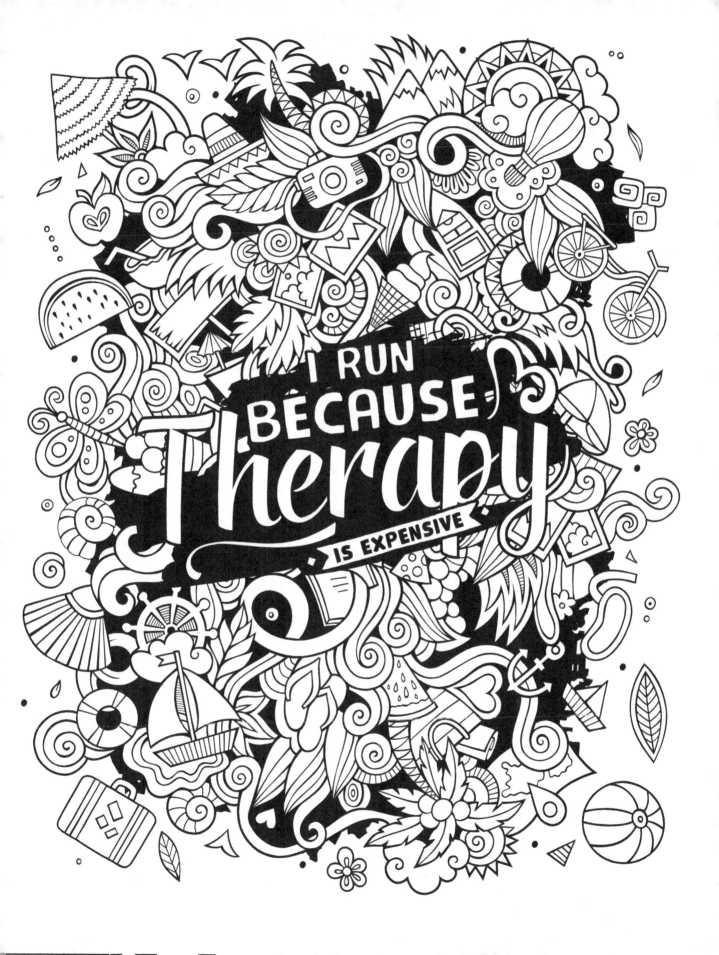

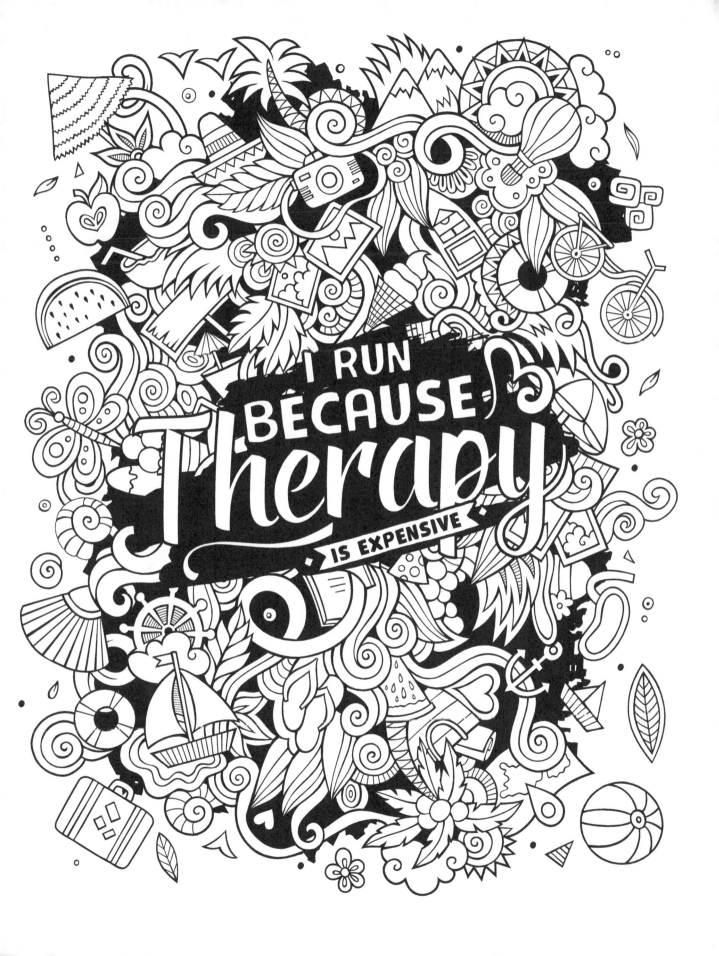

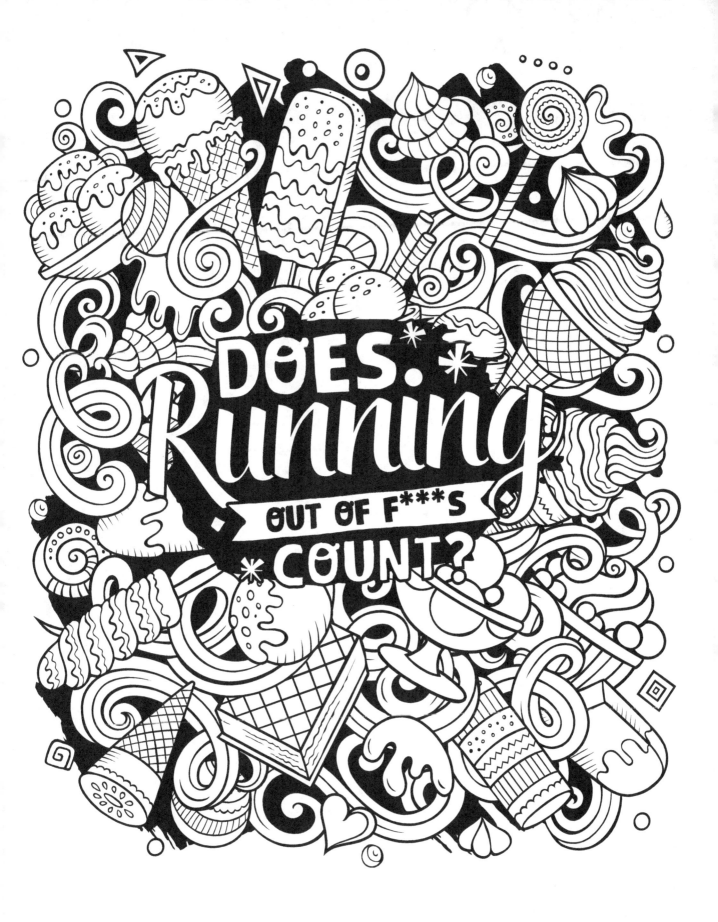

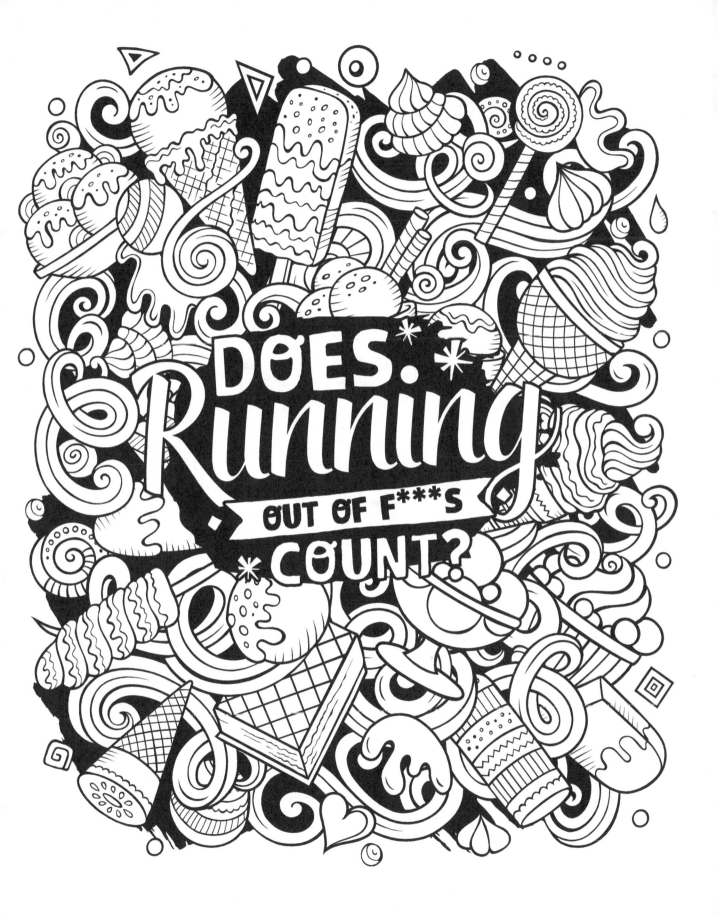

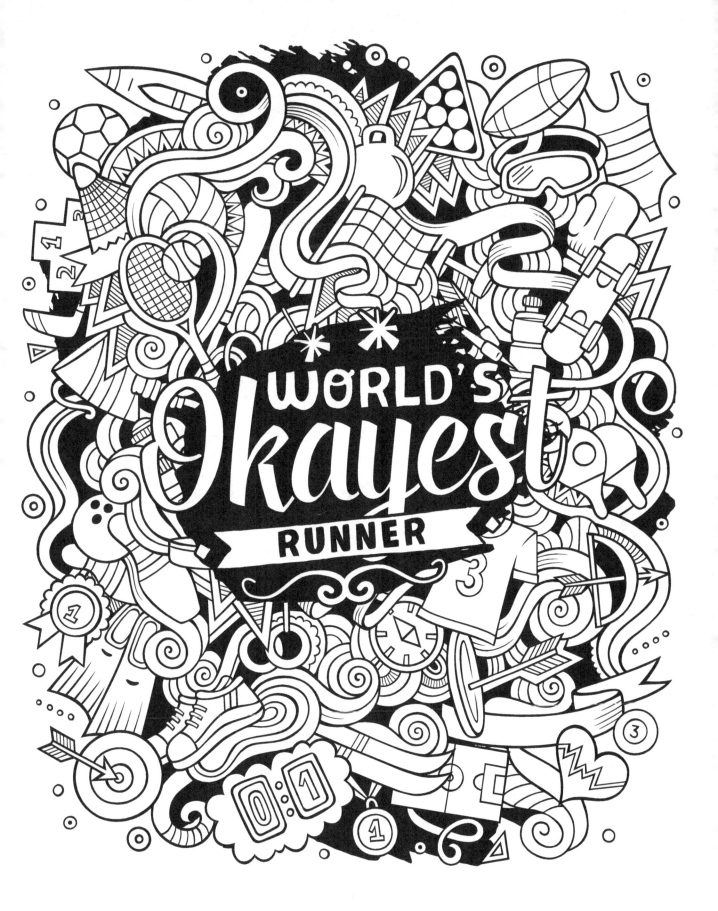

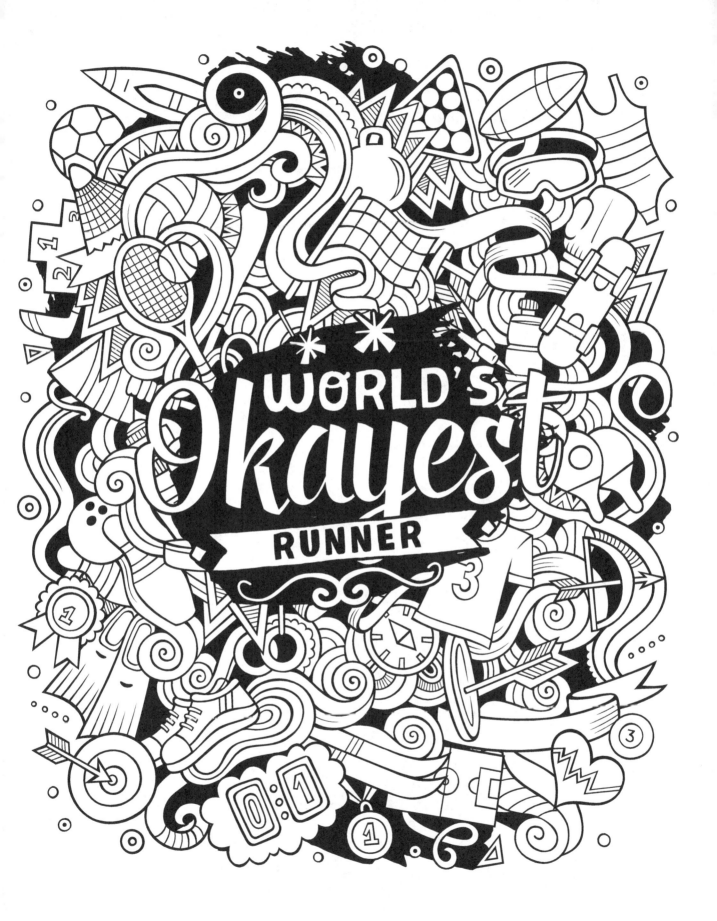

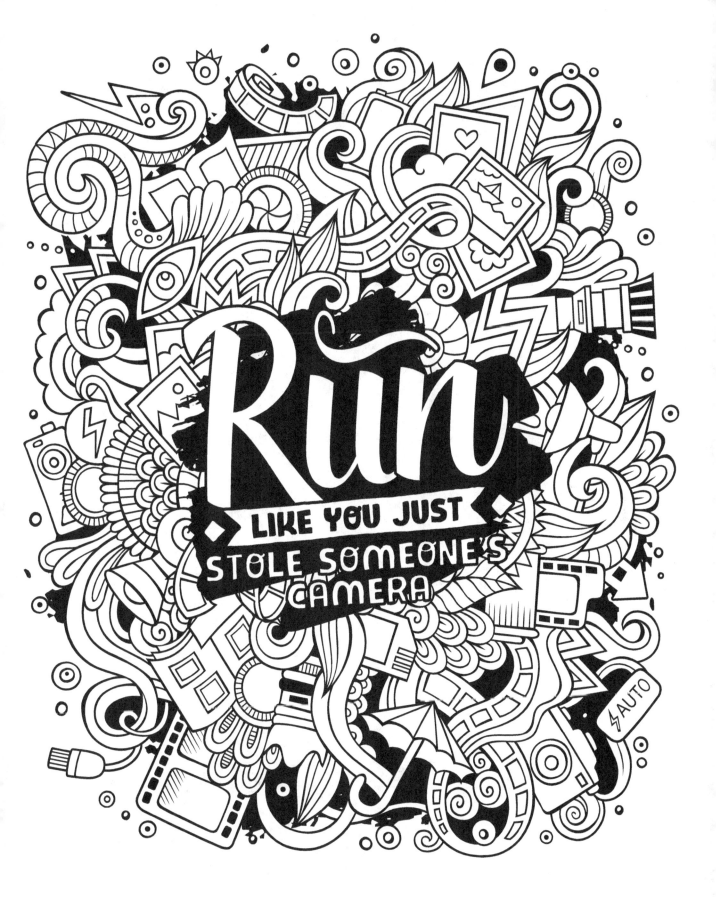

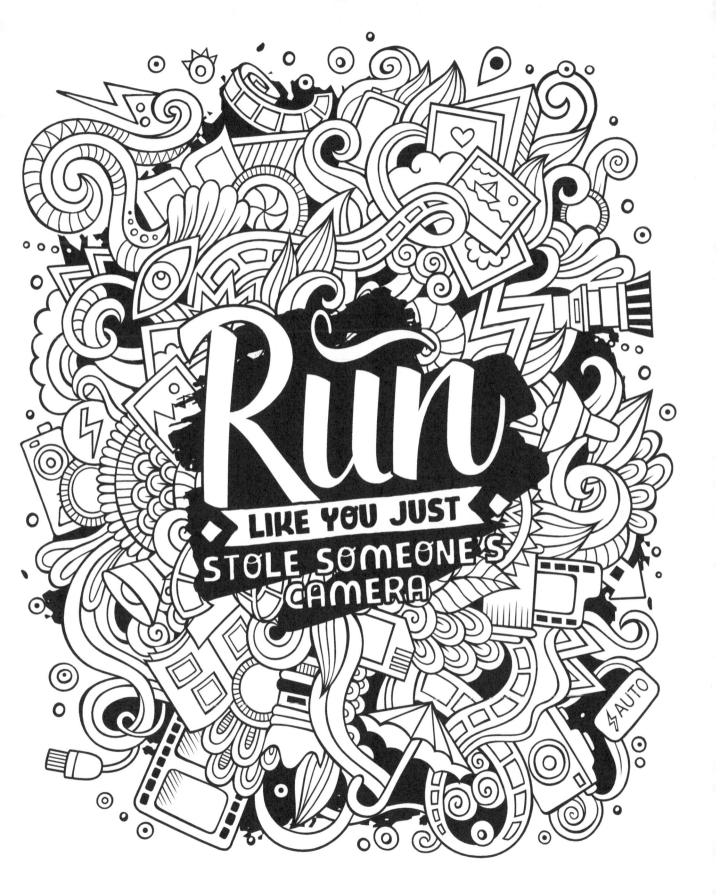

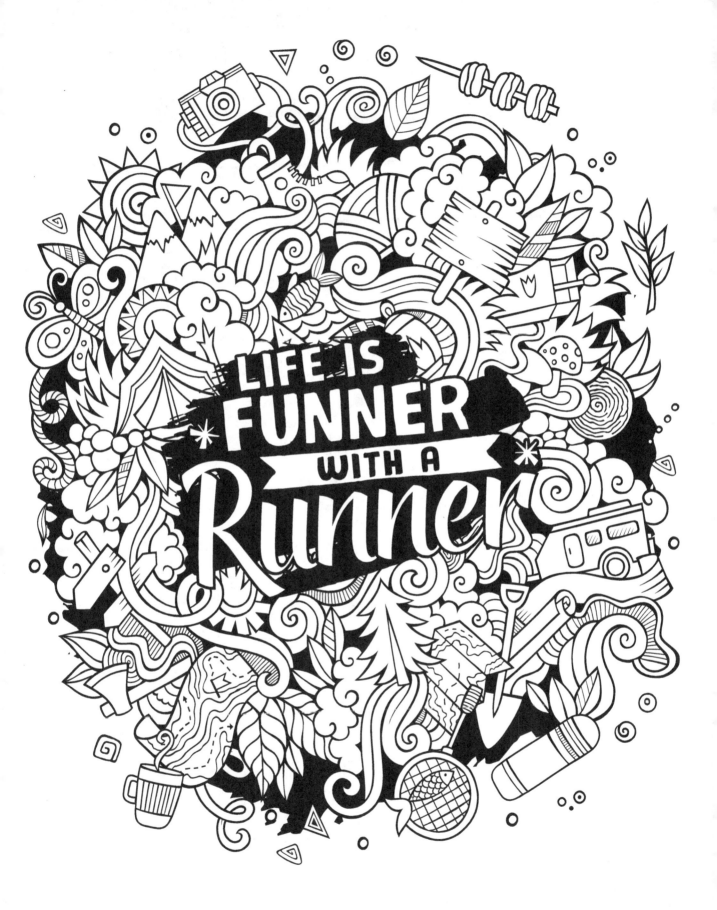

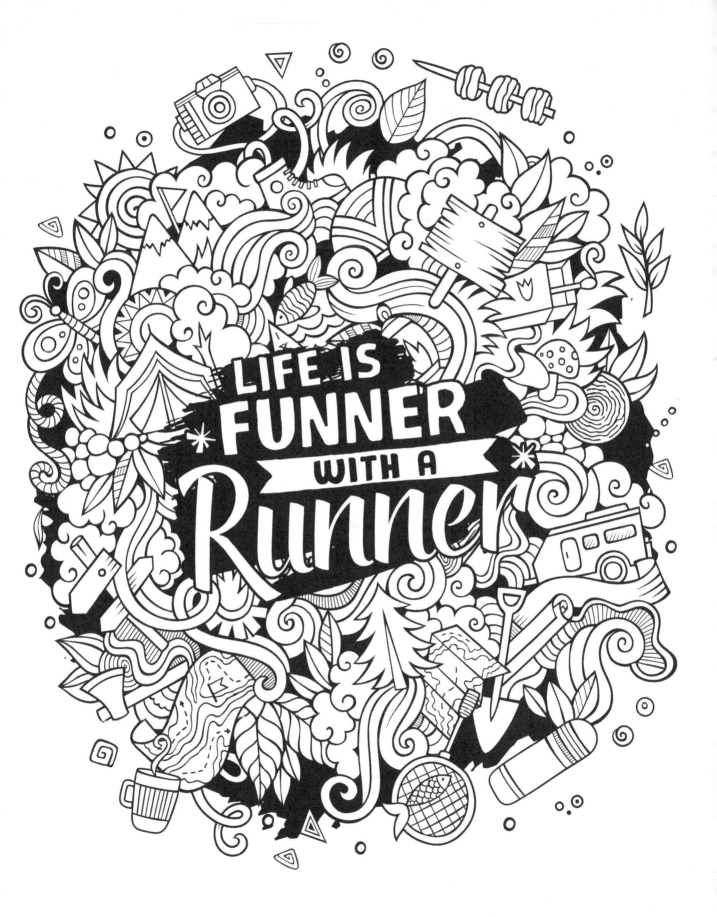

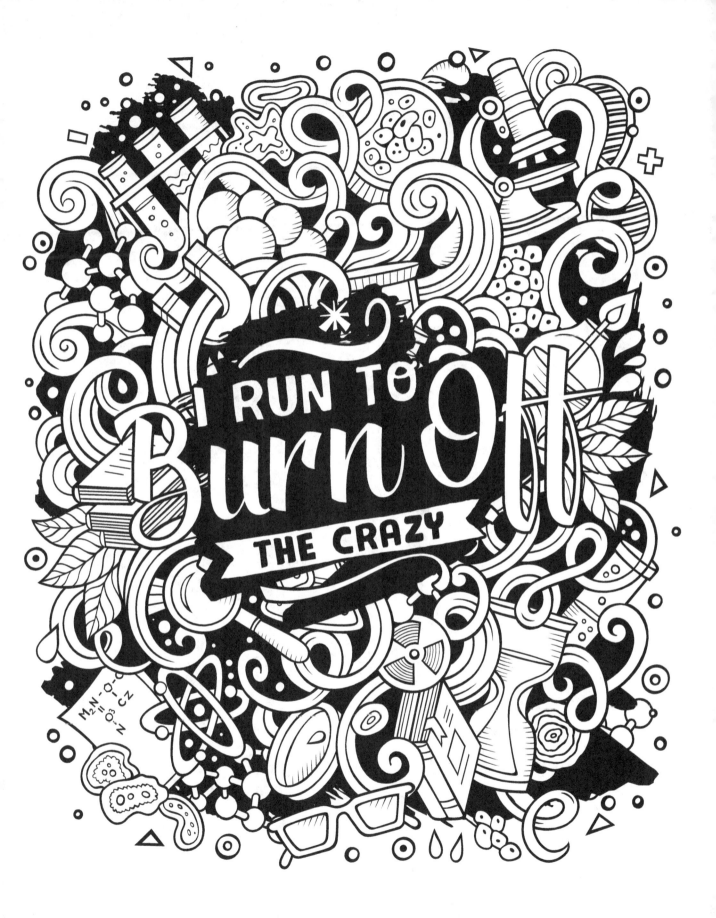

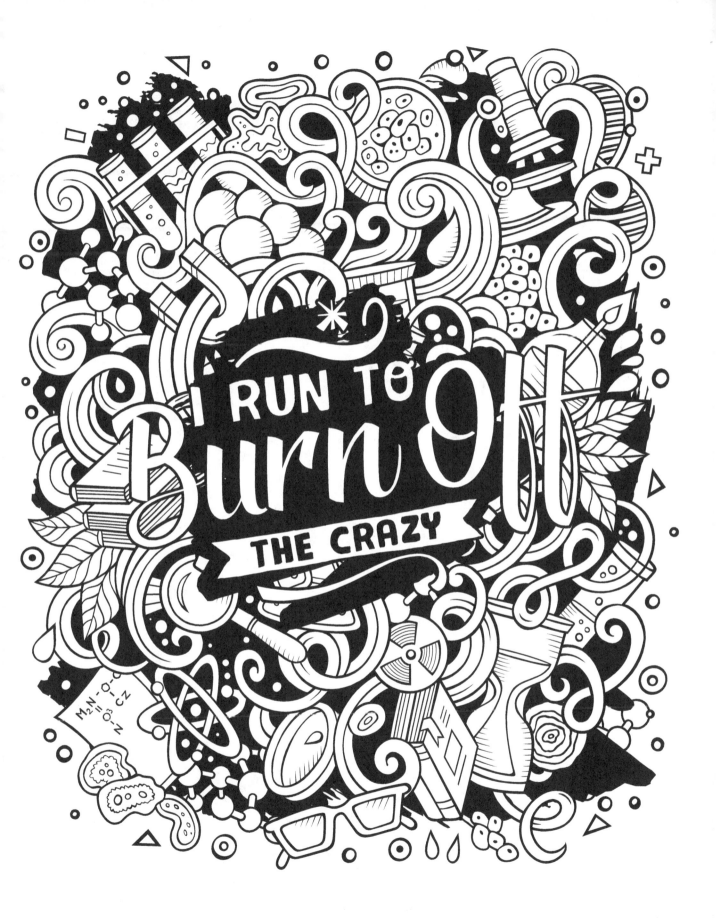

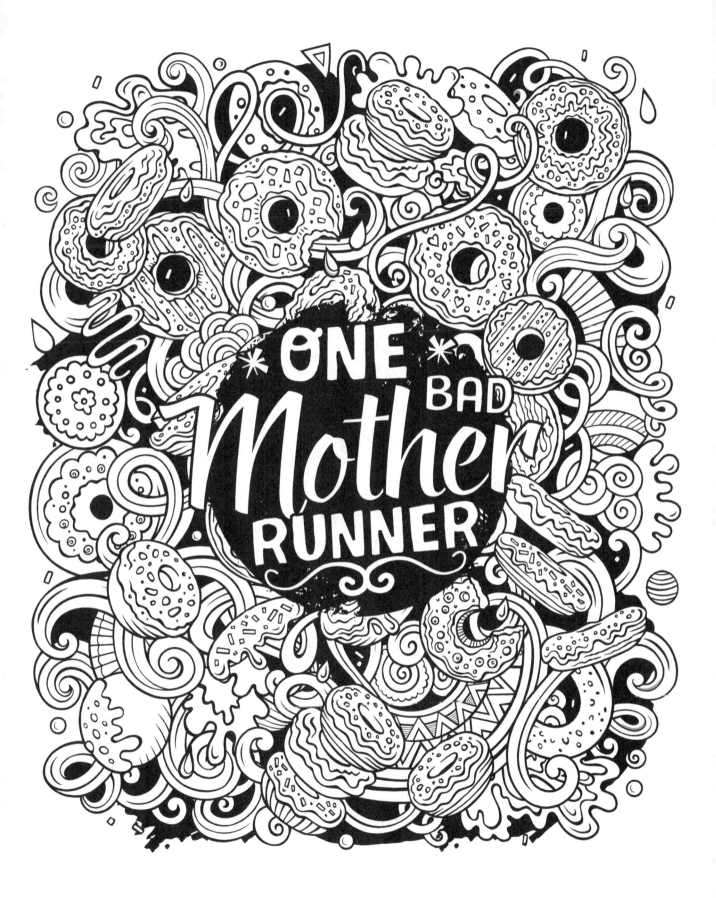

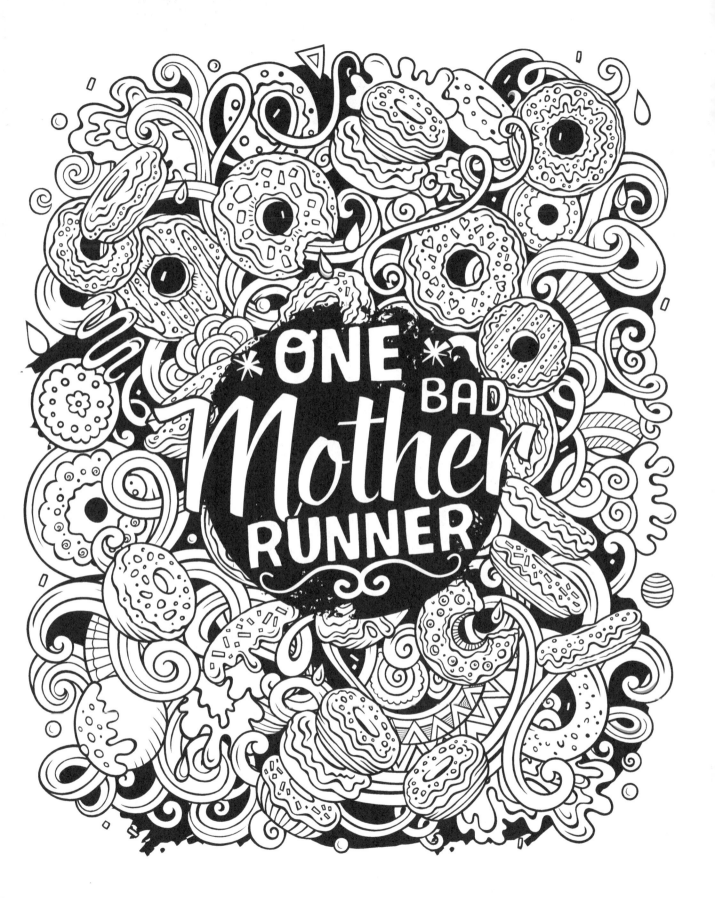

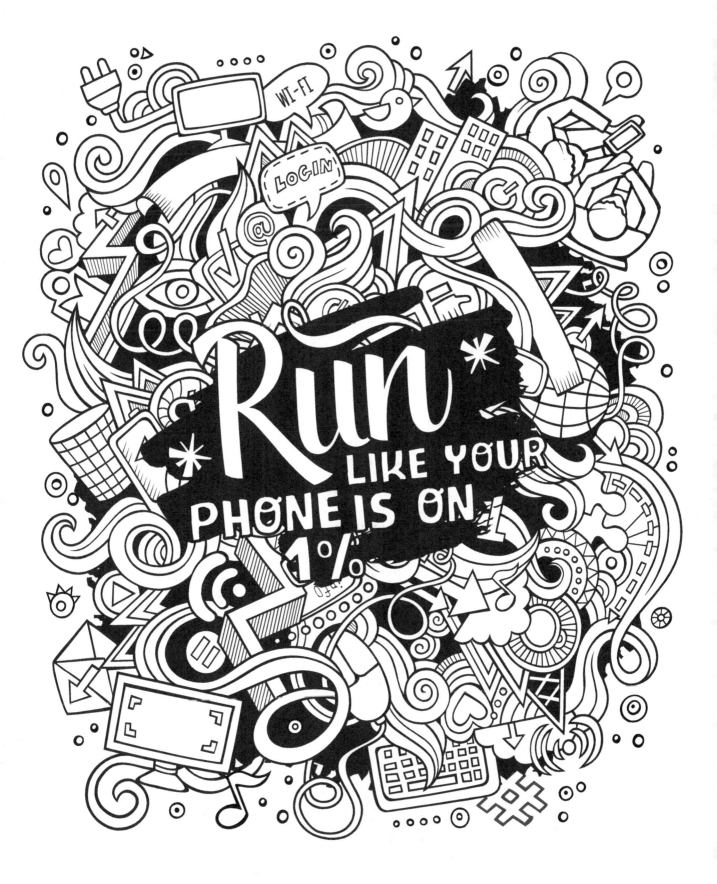

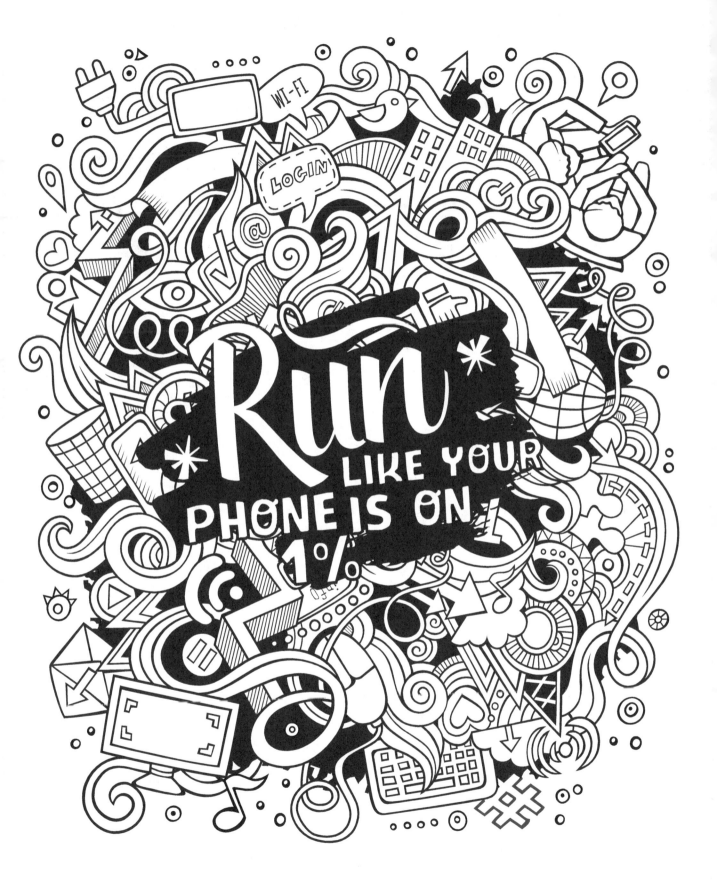

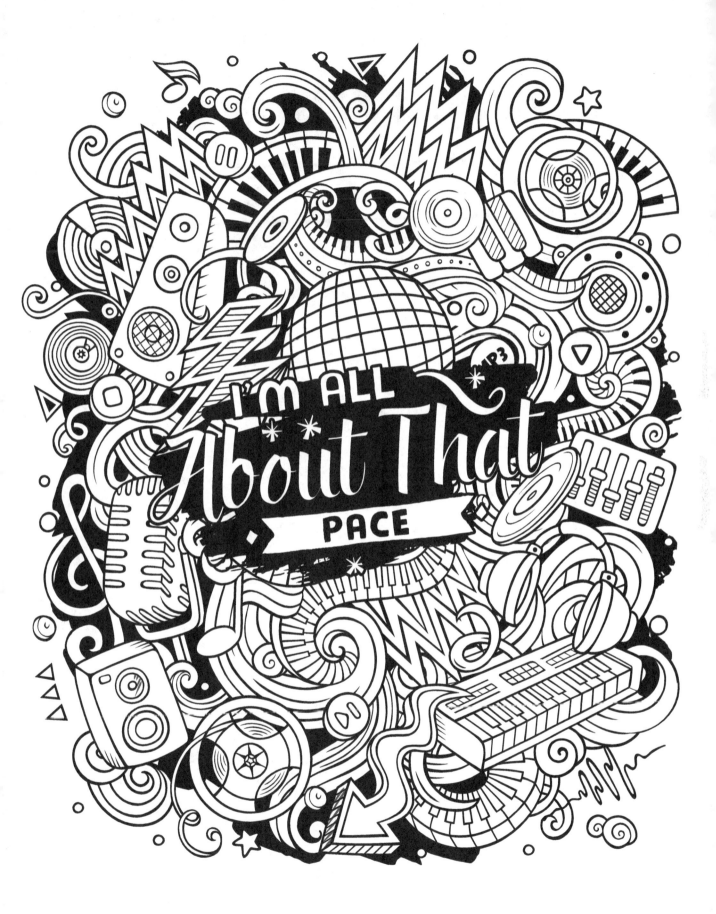

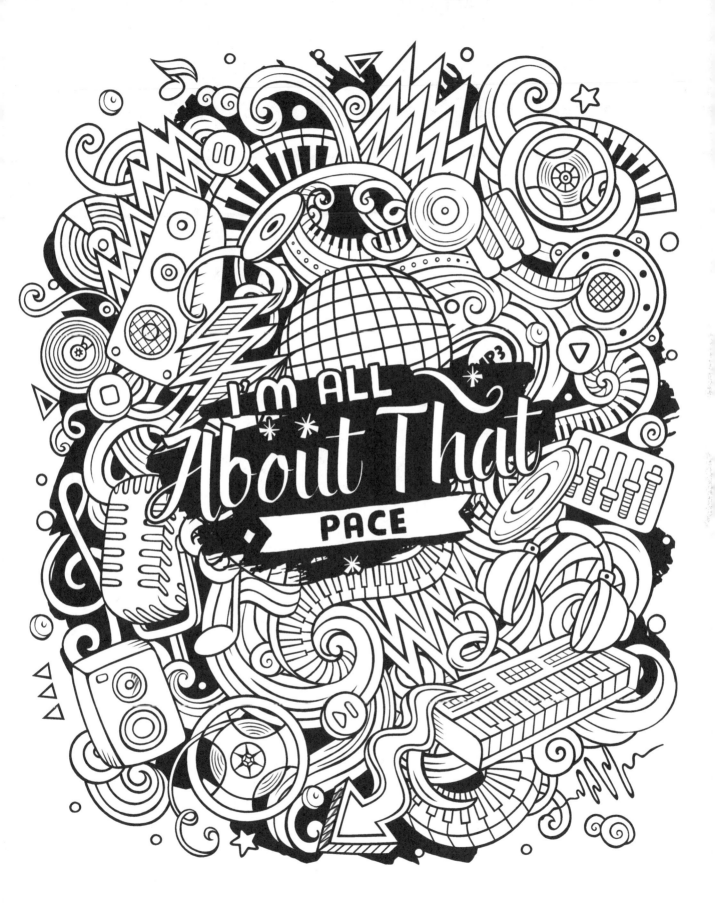

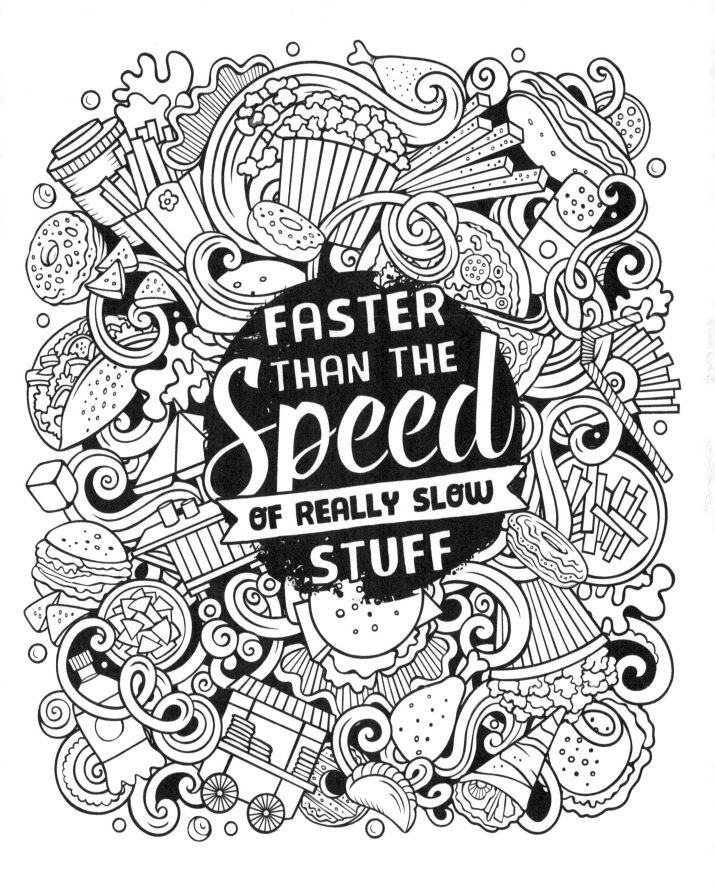

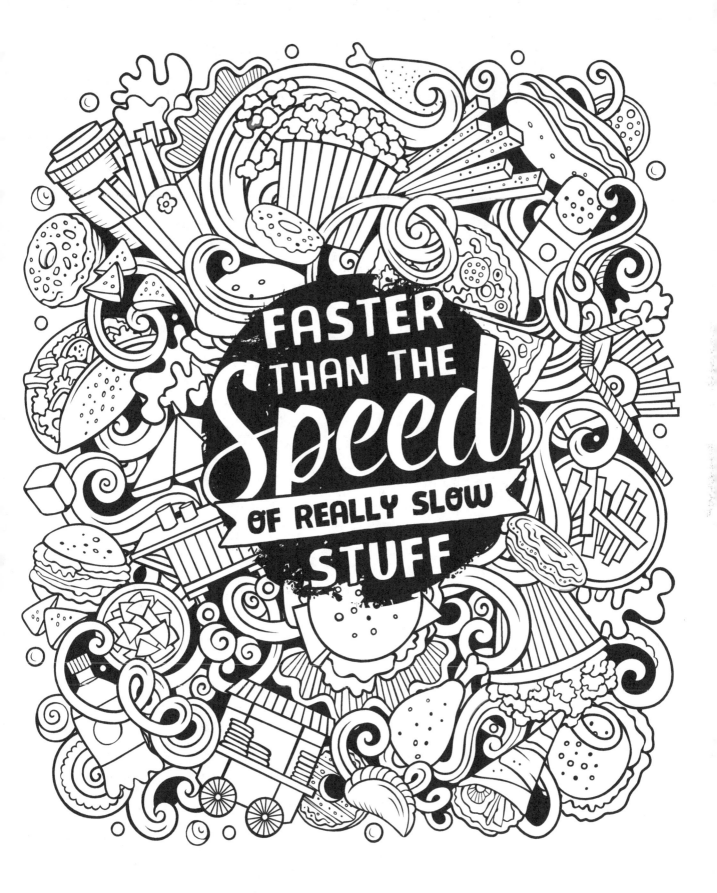

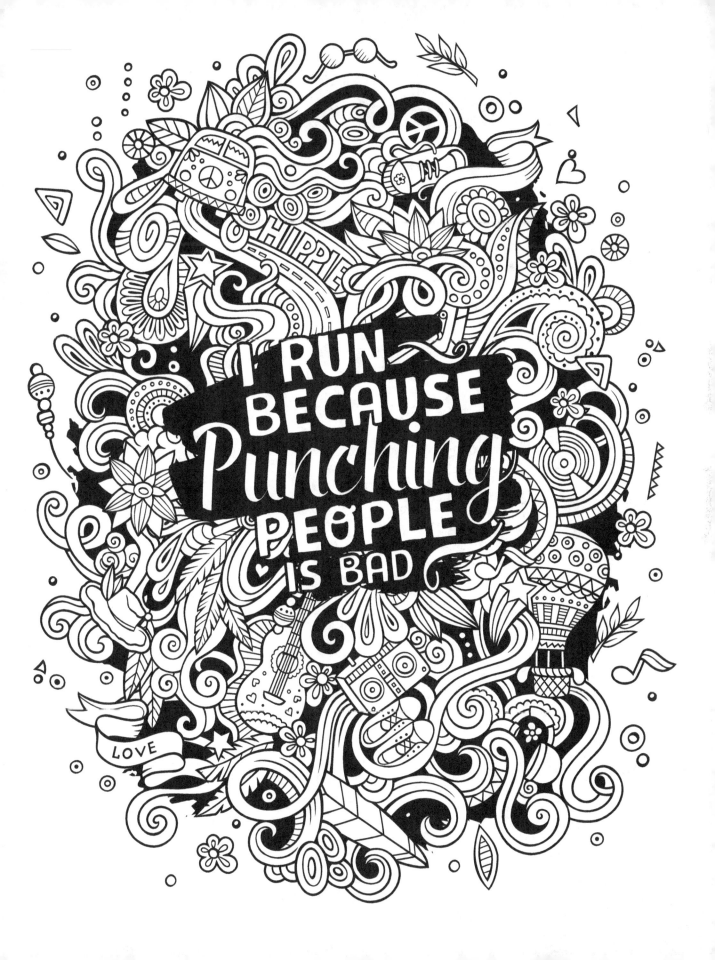

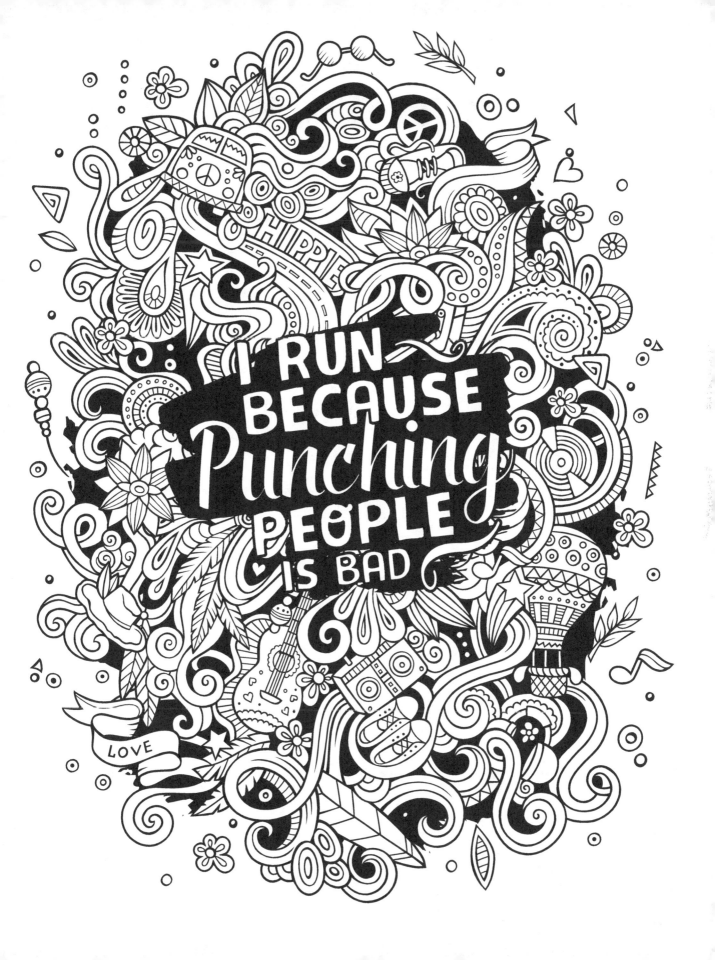

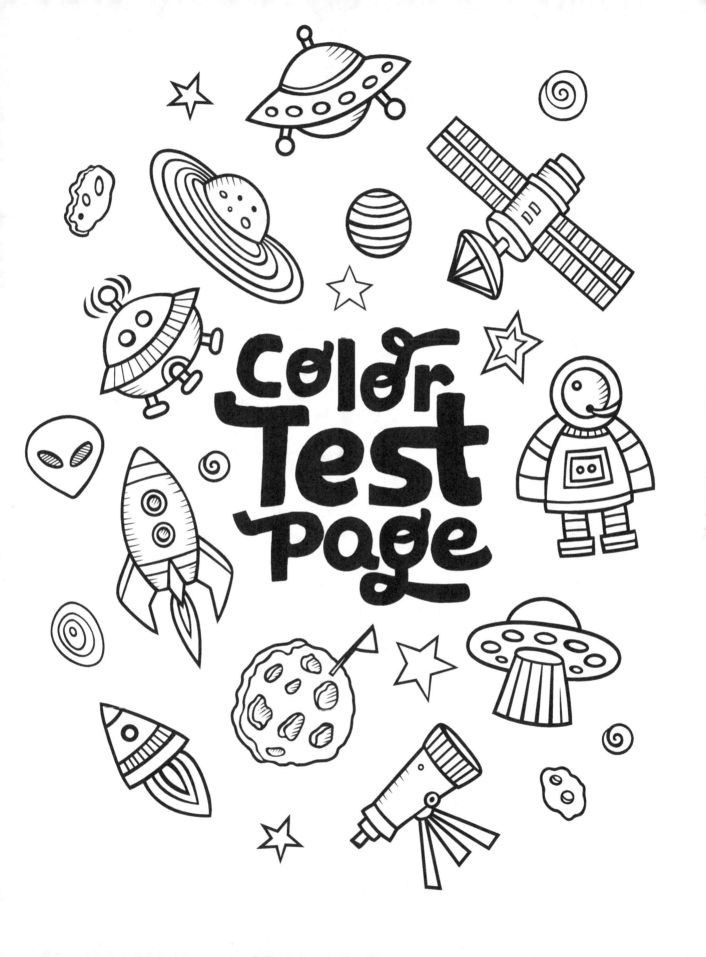

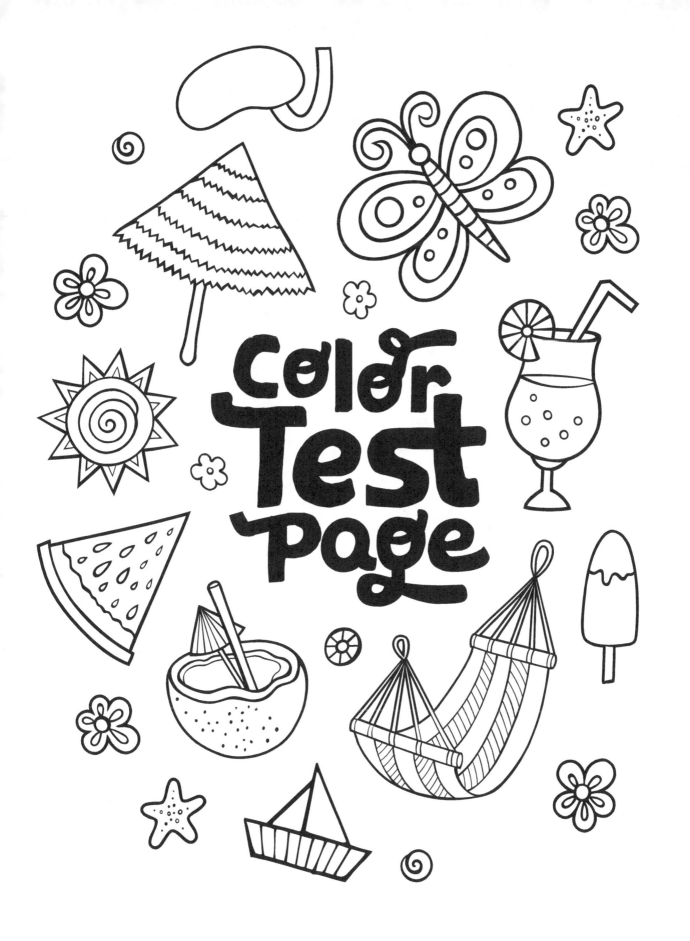

Made in United States
Troutdale, OR
07/04/2024